Branching Out

A Veteran's and Greenhorn's Guide to Successful
Branch Office Set-up, Management and Operations

By
Dr. Robert T. Berry

Dedicated to June

Photos:
Cover Photo: Dogwood tree branching out
This Page: American Redbud, branching out
Next Page: Hackberry branching out
Contents Page: Hellebores branching out

Copyright 2018
Robert T. Berry
All rights reserved

No part of this book may be reproduced in any manner without written permission, except in the case of brief quotations incorporated in critical articles and reviews and work in the public domain.

Made in the United States of America

About the author:

After a four-year active duty stint in the military, Bob Berry started his private practice career for an engineering consulting firm headquartered in Kansas City, Missouri. During his first 14 years there, he served as project engineer, project manager, director of business development and vice president. During that period, he worked with a number of the firm's branch offices primarily in the areas of sales and marketing. Then, for the next 18 years, he moved his career and family and opened and ran a branch office for the company. He retired after 32 years with the firm and now works part time as an adjunct professor for the Missouri University of Science and Technology teaching business negotiations, project management and construction management, among other courses. He also conducts seminars and short courses for industry, plays golf, goes fishing, reads and writes. He lives in St. Louis with his wife, June. His other books in print include:

"Mud, Blood and Strawberries", The Illustrated Diary of Corporal Walter L. Strawhun, 1st Division, American Expeditionary Force, 1917-1919, ISBN-13: **978-1986267809**

"Crossings", War Memories of Major Jerome T. Berry and the 19th Engineer Regiment (Combat) in North Africa, Sicily and Italy, 1940 – 1945, ISBN-13: **978-1987764345**

"Immigrant Chronicles" The Colonization of America by Our Immigrant Ancestors, ISBN-13: **978-1717288059**

Contents

INTRODUCTION 5

CHAPTER 1 – WHY OPEN A BRANCH OFFICE? 9

CHAPTER 2 – OK, WHERE? 25

CHAPTER 3 -- WHO? 33

CHAPTER 4 – GOALS AND OBJECTIVES OF A BRANCH OFFICE 41

CHAPTER 5 – DOING WORK 53

CHAPTER 6 – SELLING WORK 62

CHAPTER 7 - ORGANIZING 73

CHAPTER 8 – MEASURING PERFORMANCE 79

CHAPTER 9 – QUALITY CONTROL 82

CHAPTER 10 – RISK MANAGEMENT 85

BOB'S TOP TEN 88

Introduction

The next time you are driving around, notice how many branches there are in your city. There are branch restaurants, branch banks, branch accounting firms, branch stock brokerage firms, branch engineering firms, branch management consulting firms, branch real estate companies, branch public relations firms and branch architectural firms, among dozens of others. Some companies have a business model that maximizes branch offices to make it convenient for their customers. My bank has a branch "office" within the grocery store that we frequent. And, the grocery store is also a branch.

Our whole world is filled with branches. Branch gas stations, branch automobile dealers, branch auto parts stores, branch grocery stores and, even, branch discount golf shops. Think about universities who used to have small, medium or large campuses. Now, most universities have branch campuses located all over their region.

Opening a new branch office or a new store or a new bank branch or a new college branch campus is an everyday occurrence. One of my daughters is a "branch manager". She is the pastor of a small, new church that is a "branch" church of a bigger church a few miles away. Many churches are, in fact, branches of a denomination headquartered hundreds of miles away. My other daughter works in a branch office of a major, national real-estate company.

This book, I hope, might end up in a branch store or two of a major, national book store company. Wouldn't that be nice? Ok, you get the picture.

We see a new restaurant going into an area and we often might wonder how long it will last. Restaurants are notorious for having a glorious beginning and, then, failing after a few years. Or, sometimes having a terrible beginning and then failing after just a few weeks. Although we probably don't think of branch offices that way, my guess is that more of them end up failing than restaurants do.

Branch offices fail for many reason: poor office management, poor support from back at HQ, lack of a vision or objectives, poor organization or lack of information as to how well the office is doing or not doing. I think that most of the time, the branch office fails because the wrong person is running it or the person is not incentivized properly. But, that, of course, is the responsibility of the executive management of your firm. They are the ones who pick branch managers and decide whether and how to incentivize them, or not.

A company is normally started by one or two ingenious people with a great idea or a great invention and a lot of guts. Those one or two people have created a unique culture as well as a new company. Think Facebook or Microsoft or Ford or Amazon. As their firm grows and prospers, there seems to be a need for their service or product in far-away places and the one or two partners are also wanting some more revenue as well as some more profit to bring home. By now, they're looking at expensive colleges for their kids. So, they open their first branch.

But, there are often a lot of failures with that first branch. The partners are unable to transfer the culture that made their company prosper. They may be unable to fire up the new office manager or they are unable to realize the big profits that they were hoping and planning for. They have trouble selling work and then wonder why it was so hard in this new city. It must be the location, right?

However, I also see hundreds of branch offices that thrive and do great. Why do some fail and others succeed?

I know of a branch office that did so well, it became the new headquarters of the firm. The branch office made more money than the "mother" office and the branch manager was promoted to become CEO. He promptly moved the HQ to his city. That's success. But, that kind of success is rare.

I know of another instance where there was suddenly an opening for the COO of the company and a branch office partner, who, by the way, wasn't doing all that well as a branch manager, was promoted and moved back to take over the running of the company. Did that happen because he did such a great job running his far-away branch? No, in fact, the firm didn't even know the financials of the office because it was not a profit center. He got promoted because he was the only one of the partners that didn't have some political baggage. He was the dark-horse, far-away candidate that got the job and became managing partner and president.

If you have branch offices that are doing great, then you, or at least your branch managers, are doing some things right. But, you may have some offices that aren't doing so well. Or, maybe you have yet to open your first branch. Or, you have opened an office or two and they haven't done well and they are now just a vague but painful memory.

I have lots of stories of offices that are vague and painful memories. The really sad thing is that those offices cost a **lot** of money to open. Money was spent on doing research in the new area; money was spent hiring or moving an office manager there; money was spent on office leases and furniture and stationary and business cards and advertising and computers and travel – lots of travel. And, as we all know, travel continues to get more and more expensive.

Not only did your firm perhaps spend a lot of money on your new office, it spent a lot of: time, attention, emotional currency, sleepless nights, raging headaches and deep anxieties. But it doesn't have to be that way.

This book will give you some insights into lots of do's and don'ts regarding opening and running a branch office. It is written for CEO's and COO's and partners and those contemplating being a branch office manager (BOM). It's also written for those who have had failures in opening an office but have not given up.

It's written for sole-proprietors, partnerships, corporations and ESOP's as well as for real small companies and very large companies – the thoughts are pretty much the same.

You will likely not agree with a lot of what I propose. That's ok. But, I contend, that the more of this advice you take, the more successful your branches will be.

We are going to talk about *Why* we even want to open an office. And, risk, and quality control and selling work and doing work. And, most of all, we're going to consider *who* you should choose to run your branch office and even, some thoughts on *where* to locate one.

Along the way, I summarize a few of my points with a few Brilliant Advise Boxes.

Have fun.

I want to say "thanks" to all of the branch managers out there who took on the odds against them by agreeing to run a branch office. I also want to say "thanks" to Joel and Doug who encouraged me to grab the golden ring when it came around and to Dave and Newt who accepted the risks and sanctioned the adventure.

And, of course, "thanks" to all of my friends and colleagues over the years who worked for me in our little experiment. And, of course, to our clients who gambled a little when they hired us and the home office folks who encouraged us and helped us.

Chapter 1 – Why Open a Branch Office? (Prestige, of course.)

So, you want to open a branch office? Have you asked yourself why? There are a lot of reasons to open a branch office – many good reasons and many bad reasons. Let's talk about the bad reasons first. If bad reasons are the only reasons you have to open a branch office, then you might want to reconsider.

I suggest that you save yourself a lot of time and trouble and money and heartache and days away from your family and poor hiring decisions if you only have bad reasons. Forget it. Let's take a look at some *bad* reasons.

Prestige. Bad reason number 1 is Prestige. Hey, no kidding, multiple locations look great on your tombstone ads. Your company brochure has a new kind of image when you list multiple locations; it gives a sense of success and accomplishment to your corporate letterhead. It looks even better when they are sexy locations like, say, South Beach or Manhattan or Pasadena or La Jolla. Or, even better, London or Paris or Dubai looks great on your website. It tells everyone, especially your family members, clients and friends, that you are successful and making lots of money – right? Plus, it's great fun to imagine that your competitors are green with envy that you are so successful that you have an office in Nice – nice.

If you're the CEO or the COO or the CAO or the VP of Marketing, it looks great for you to have multiple branch offices. But, keep in mind that you are the one who's bonus and next salary increase will be affected most by the success of the office. And, keep in mind that you are not the one moving there or having to manage this new venture.

There have been many branch offices opened just to advertise that your company is successful, regardless of whether they are successful or not. Prestige.

But, we have to ask some questions here. Are they bringing in *new* business? Just as important, are they earning revenue? Are those offices profitable? Are they enhancing your company's reputation? Oops – you may not even know if they are making money or not, if your accounting system isn't set up right.

I know a company that opened a branch office in Washington DC. The office staff consisted of two assistants and an office manager. None of the staff were billable. The office was large and nicely appointed and was in a high-rent building. It had beautiful, clubby mahogany paneling, plush carpeting and big windows looking out over the Potomac.

But, the office brought in no appreciable amount of work, never made any sales and did not contribute to the company bottom line. They were there for the *prestige* of having an office in DC.

The office manager had dozens of photos on his vanity wall showing autographed photos of him with various presidents and senators and admirals and generals and whoever. But there was no evidence that any of those photo-ops represented projects won or completed. The office manager was a regular member of The Army and Navy Club and hob-knobbed with all of the important and not-so-important generals and admirals. He even took me to lunch there once – we had Navy bean soup, I remember.

The reason that the office was there was that the CEO wanted the *prestige* of having a DC office, regardless of the cost. Since the CEO knew that the office couldn't and wouldn't contribute to the bottom line, the CEO just put all of the costs of the DC office into corporate overhead so that no one would ever know how much it cost. Of course, putting the costs in corporate overhead, meant that not only the headquarters, but all of the firm's branch offices and divisions had to share in the costs of the DC office through corporate allocations. We will talk about that later.

One could argue that the DC office sold work for the overall company and may have contributed to sales. In fact, the CEO made sure to credit the DC office whenever a sale was made to any agency of the Federal government even when the DC office had nothing to do with it.

One could easily imagine that the membership costs of the Army and Navy Club was a small price to pay for all of the contacts there that, of course, resulted in all of the firm's Federal work. But, it would be a big stretch to say that the DC office benefited any of the branch offices, yet they paid their unfair share of the DC office costs in their allocated overheads.

The trouble with "prestige" is that few CEO's will ever admit that they want to open an office because of prestige. Other reasons will be cited, such as markets, or clients or growth, or circumstances or, "the I-know-a-great-guy" reason, or whatever. So, you have to dig deep and ask yourself carefully if prestige is your main reason or not. In my opinion, it should have no bearing on your decision – prestige can cost a LOT of money – your money.

Of course, if you are the CEO, you can decide to open a new branch anywhere you want, including Washington DC. That is your prerogative and, the Navy Bean soup is pretty good there. It's also largely your money that you're spending.

Location. Bad reason number 2 is Location. There are a lot of great places to have an office. And, there are a lot of places that don't seem to be a "prestigious" location for an office. Although I really like these locations, I would say that having a branch office in Wichita, Spokane, Omaha, Chattanooga, Buffalo or Birmingham doesn't add too much prestige to your letterhead. However, that's not the case with locations like: Las Vegas, Orlando, San Diego, Austin or South Beach, and Washington, DC, of course.

I know of a medium-sized company who had a few partners, one of which wanted to move to Miami when he retired. So, he convinced the other partners to let him open a Miami office a few years before his retirement date so that he could warm up, so to speak, to the Miami area before the big day. His plan was to spend a few months setting up the office and then a year or two down there to run it and then to retire there.

Once set up, he would move to Miami, on the company's nickel of course, run the office for a year or two and then retire. Otherwise, if he retired and *then* moved to Miami, he'd have to pay for it. This meant that the partner spent much of his time during the next many months going back and forth to Miami, leasing building space, buying and renting office equipment, hiring staff and setting up the new branch office. So, he split his time between opening the new office and his duties back at headquarters, to the detriment of both the new Miami office, as well as the company.

Finally, the new Miami office opened with few staff and even less work. Their billable time was non-existent and the office staff got pretty bored pretty fast. Gradually, the headquarters was able to send some work their way and eventually they started getting their own work.

Of course, the company added to their *prestige* by listing another office in a sexy location. And, the partner got a whole lot of paid vacations going back and forth before he actually moved there. During his frequent trips to Miami (all of which were paid for by the company, of course) he was able to hunt for a house, join a country club, and scout out all sorts of fun places that he and his wife could frolic on company time.

Since this venture was a fairly unique situation in the company, the partner convinced the other partners that they should not have the new Miami office be a profit center. The costs of the office, including the salaries and overheads of the office and his costs traveling back and forth, were all assigned as corporate overheads so the other partners were never aware of how much or how little money the office was making and, of course, losing.

Over the next couple of years, the Miami office managed to sell some work but ended up having to send a lot of it back to headquarters and they got a bad reputation in the area because of the shoddy work that they did do. And, they didn't get the respect of the folks in headquarters who then were reluctant to send work to them. (We'll talk about quality control in Chapter 9).

Brilliant Advise Box

Branch offices must be a profit center on day one. Do everyone a favor, including your executive principals, your new branch manager and all of your practice managers and make sure your CFO sets up your new branch as soon as it opens – or before.

The situation got so bad that the company asked the partner to retire early and it had to spend money and corporate energy to "straighten up the mess" that he had created. But, it was too late. Although the partner had a lot of ability, there was too much damage done prior to his move there to bail out the office. It suffered from a bad reputation, below average employees with no incentive and a huge cultural difference between the swinging, Latin-minded South Beach area and the Midwest where headquarters was.

Eventually the office folded. How much had that venture cost the company? No one will ever know as the costs and overheads and poorly executed projects were are all buried in corporate accounts – they didn't want to know.

In Chapter 2 we will talk about *where* to open an office. But, if your reason to open an office is based on a great location or prestige, you are making the wrong decision.

Circumstances. Bad reason number 3 is that circumstances dictate opening a new office. Yes, a lot of branch offices are opened because you somehow get a nice project in a city where you heretofore haven't done much work. There's an attitude that there seems to be a lot of work coming up with this new client so, since you are already working there anyway and have a "base load" of work, you decide to go ahead and set up a branch office there. Plus, the city seems to be growing and has potential for a lot of work that your firm does. Thousands of branch offices have been set up around the world in this way.

You pick a person on your staff that will be a key person on the new project and offer him/her the chance to move to the new city and "open an office". Never mind that this person has a family in the headquarters city and their spouse has a good job there, and their kids are in school there, and all four of the grandparents live nearby. Never mind that the costs to the company in moving expenses, office set up and hundreds of other costs might never be offset by the profits of this new project, especially considering that you got the new project in the first place without an office there.

I know a New England-based company that got a nice new project in Austin, Texas. They had joint-ventured with another firm that was headquartered in Austin but that firm had no expertise in doing the new project. Since Austin (and Texas in general) was booming (and still is), the New England-based company decided to open an Austin office but to do it on the cheap with as little money as possible.

So, with the cooperation of the joint venture company, they had a phone installed that sat on the desk of the receptionist of the Austin-based JV partner. She would answer that phone with the name of the New England-based company rather than her own company. (Although, it seldom rang.) They had mail delivered to a PO box and printed letterhead with the PO box and the new phone number.

They sent two guys down to do the project and to start and run the "Austin Office" despite the fact that neither of them agreed to move to Austin and, in fact, planned to *not* move to Austin. They worked at desks in the JV partner's offices.

The next issue of the company's quarterly magazine showed the new Austin Office on the cover and highlighted both of the guys who were there to run it, as well as the project. Of course, it was very prestigious to have an office in the fast-growing Austin area. Unfortunately, by the time that the magazine came out and got in the mail, the project was finished and both guys had come back home. They never intended to move to Austin and, in fact, worked 16-hour days during their stay there to finish the work as soon as possible so that they could get home to their families.

> **Brilliant Advise Box**
>
> Starting a new branch office just because you got a new project with a new client in a new city – regardless of how lucrative the new client and the new city seem to be, is usually a bad idea.

This actually happened and damaged the reputation of the firm not only in Austin and Texas in general but nationally for the firm.

In other cases, firms promise to open an office if they get a nice new project in a new location. Sometimes, someone gets a little carried away and makes a promise in the proposal or interview or over lunch that if they are selected for the work, they will open an office there and do some or most of the work there. And, often, that "someone" doesn't have the authority or prior permission to even make that promise. Can you believe that ever happens?

Has this happened to your firm? Thousands of branch offices have been opened that way and most end up failing. The office was poorly conceived and perhaps doesn't have board approval and little planning or market research has occurred. There is no one to open it or run it. The project may not even be big enough to justify it or, if it is, there is no staff to do it.

Circumstances are not a good reason to open an office. It's true that circumstances can be a reasonable catalyst that encourages planning and research and justifies opening an office for the right reason, but please, or my sake, don't justify a poorly planned and executed new branch office with circumstances alone.

Marketing Success. Bad reason number 4 is that your new office will result in a lot of new work. Some believe the myth that since your firm is such a great company, if you only had an office in that city, you would have tons of work.

It is certainly easier to sell work to a local client if you have a local office than to sell work to a client if you don't have a local office. Or, is it? Many folks in headquarters think that if they only had an office in Dallas, for example, they could get work in Dallas. But let's take a look at that way of thinking.

First, is it true that the clients in Dallas tend to only hire firms that have a significant local presence? You will need to do some research on this and ask some questions. If it is true, then you need to find out if those clients have significant work coming up, right? You may, indeed, find a client who might tell you that if you had a local office you would be considered for work, but you also need to make sure that the client does, indeed, have work to give you.

Most agencies and companies hire firms that they trust. They trust that the firm will be honest with them, and provide value for the services they provide and that they will come running when there's a problem – as there often is. If a firm is not local, it's much harder for them to come running – at least with the urgency that is generally expected. This is one big reason agencies and companies hire local firms: they want fast response when they call. There is also pressure from local forces to hire local firms. The local firms will do all they can to keep out the competition.

> **Brilliant Advise Box**
>
> Clients hire firms because they trust them more than their competition. They trust you to come through for them, to give them the expertise that you say you have, and to give them value for your fee or price. They mostly trust that by hiring you, they will look good to their boss.

I remember a case in a location where a big, new firm without a local office was chosen for a nice, big project for the city there. Several of the local firms who thought (rightly so) that they were just as qualified as the out-of-town firm, banded together and went to the city fathers with a spreadsheet showing the amount of local taxes they paid each year compared to the *zero* taxes paid by the big, swanky out-of-town firm. The city fathers overturned their selection. In that case, "local" won out over expertise.

But, the good news is that clients also hire firms because of their expertise. If you have a specific, somewhat unique problem, they will hire the firm who they trust can best solve their problem, much like people who want the best doctor they can find to solve their unique heart problem – regardless of where they are located.

> **Brilliant Advise Box**
>
> If a client will hire you to do work without having a local office, why would you want to open one there? A branch office exists to sell work to clients who must have their work done, at least partly, by a local office.

It's a mistake to think that opening a new branch office will lead to a lot of marketing success there. Although that might happen, normally it doesn't. Remember, clients hire firms that they trust and that have the expertise that they need to solve their problem. If they can do that by hiring local firms, they generally will.

Bring in business that you would not otherwise get?
This bad reason is really a subset of Bad Reason Number 4, above so we will call it Bad Reason Number 4b. Clients might be categorized in two ways: 1) those that will hire you regardless of where the work will be done – they don't care where you are; and, 2) those customers that will normally only hire firms with a significant local presence with expectations that most, or at least, some of the work will be done locally.

If you have clients of the first type, that is, clients who don't really care where the work will be done, there is no reason to open an office there. I know a firm that used to get significant work from the city of Knoxville even though they didn't have an office within 500 miles of that city.

If you are already getting work there, then why open an office there? They are obviously hiring you because they trust you more than the local folks, so don't rock the boat. But, be prepared for the whims of the local folks to change and bow to pressure from local firms. Because, they may change their philosophy and start only hiring local firms, especially as the local firms put more and more pressure on them to hire locally. But, if you are already getting work for that client without a local presence, then why spend the money and time and focus to open one there? (Oh, I forgot, it looks good on your letterhead.)

However, if you have targeted clients that have long-term work and who have a history of hiring a range of firms to work for them but only if they have a local presence, then you might consider opening a branch there. But, a *bad* reason to open a branch there is to get work from client(s) from whom you are already getting work without a local presence.

I know an agency that suddenly was mandated by the Federal government to spend a lot of money – around $5 billion over two decades. That agency had a written policy to *only* hire firms that had a significant local presence.

They didn't insist that firms do all of their work locally, but a firm must have had a real office with real people, some of whom were capable of doing some of their work. Once they announced their new $5 billion program, out-of-town firms flocked to town and opened offices. Some sent folks to run it from back home while others recruited and hired experienced, senior people already living there, to run their new office. Some succeeded in getting some of the work; others didn't.

Great Guy. Bad Reason Number 5. Let's see – what other bad reasons are there? Oh, yes, how about the great guy that has lots of contacts and wants to come to work for your firm but wants to live somewhere where you don't have an operation? I've seen this more than once.

This kind of thing happens all of the time, too. I know a firm who had a great employee working for them. He was smart, a great salesman, a great project manager and a real go-getter. But, his spirit wandered and he quit and went to work for another firm in a distant, far-away land. After a couple of years, he decided that he'd made a mistake and wanted to come back to the first firm but by then, his family was settled in their new home and were happy in their new schools and his wife had obtained a great job there. So, he convinced the first firm to hire him back and to open and "run" a one-man sales office focusing on selling work in the region of his home. He, of course, was never "billable" and he incurred quite a lot of travel costs as well as office overhead costs.

He worked mostly out of his home and set up an "office" with a desk and phone in his spare bedroom next to the TV and in front of the twin beds. Again, the costs of this one-man office were buried in the big division so it never showed up in any P&L statements. Oh, but wait, what about all of the work that he brought in? Actually, there wasn't any new work. There were lots and lots of opportunities for new work, but there was always some reason why the firm was not selected for it. According to the great guy, the reason was never his fault – the work was priced too high, or HQ assigned the wrong project manager or the proposal was screwed up, or whatever.

Clients who will hire you to do the work in another location, don't need a local sales guy; clients who want their work done locally, also don't need a local sales guy. It was a mess and it took over five years of agony to finally cut him loose (again). Of course, it looked prestigious in their brochures for a while.

Ok, I'm sure there are other bad reasons, but let's take a look at some good reasons.

Make more profit. Good Reason No. 1 is to make more profit. In fact, it's the only reason that makes sense to me. Those who make a decision to open a branch or regional office must understand that they must make more profit as a firm *with* the new office than they would without it. Of course, you have to have a planning horizon. You can't expect a new office to be profitable on day 1, or, even, year 1, but certainly they should be profitable by the end of 2 years.

And, I don't mean more revenue. Yes, you might sell more work and get more revenue, but if the new office is not bringing in more profit, then why are you doing it?

Consider who owns your company. If you are a sole-proprietorship, or partnership, then if a new branch office makes $1,000 of profit, (assuming all overheads are considered) then the partners get to split that $1,000. Or, if your firm is a corporation with outside stockholders, then, they also will share the extra $1,000 of profit. But, if your corporation is an employee-owned company, for example, then that $1,000 may *not* represent a true profit as compared to profit per person. In that instance, if the rest of the company made a profit of say, $10,000 per person and the new branch office made a profit of $200 per person, then, overall, the stockholder/employee-owners, *lost* money. Right?

So, your ultimate and, indeed, only reason to open a branch office is to increase profit per share or profit per owner. And, you must keep in mind that your accounting must include overheads and allocations. We'll talk a lot more about that as we go.

I say this realizing that a firm has to have a lengthy planning horizon. If you think your company will stagnate in its current headquarters location and must branch out in order to stay in business, well, then, that's different. But, consider that your branch offices may take decades to surpass the headquarters operation in profit per shareholder.

> **Brilliant Advise Box**
>
> The only good reason to open a branch office is that you believe that in the medium to long-term, the firm will make more profit per shareholder with the branch office than without it.

Good Reason No. 2 – See reason no. 1.

Of course, you can do whatever you want to do. But, your fiduciary responsibility to the shareholders of your company is to increase long-term profit per share or profit per owner. If your plan for the new branch office doesn't expect to show that in a reasonable amount of time - forget it.

Speaking of Good Reason Number 1, you have to count the beans correctly. Unless you are opening a branch office for one of the bad reasons previously discussed, then you must create a profit center for this office on day *one*. You must know, and your board must know, and the people running your new branch office must know, if they are making money or not and how much and why.

Financial data is tightly guarded in many closely held firms, but I don't see how you can expect to have a successful branch office without all key people concerned knowing what the financials are for the new branch. I define "successful" as an office that is increasing the overall profit per share of the company, if not in the beginning, at least in the medium-term.

And don't cheat. It's easy to hide low-billable people by assigning them to headquarters although they are really in the branch. I know because I've done that. Or, letting HQ pay for the relocation expenses to relocate key people to the new location even though that ought to be a branch expense. The new branch office needs to stand on their own two feet, regardless of how bad it might look at first, and do so, on day one. And, they must be able to see where "their feet are". In other words, your branch managers need to see the financials each month of their office.

I personally believe that all of your principals ought to see the financials of the whole company every month – but that is a tough nut to swallow for some. When the costs and profitability of the new branch office come out each month, it will probably end up being painful for all: those who advocated for the office; those managing the office; office employees who may know the profitability of the office; and, board members and share-holders watching their profit per share diminish. At least at first.

But, be sure you don't cheat the other way either. Make sure you don't make the branch office pay for the overheads of headquarters or other branches. For example, if the headquarters has season tickets to the local baseball team, don't allocate those costs to branch offices. Those are overhead or marketing costs for the headquarters – not the branches. If the branch offices buy tickets to their local team, then they should pay for them.

And, if you have a Washington DC office that's not making any money, don't collar your branch offices with those allocated costs. Set up your DC office as a separate profit center and allocate corporate costs to it rather than subsidize it by allocating its costs to all of your profit centers and branch offices.

Similarly, if the headquarters needs to repave their parking lot, or put on a new roof, make sure those costs are paid for by the folks in the headquarters and not those in other locations.

So, it's going to take some time for your CFO and accounting people to set up charge codes for the new office and, perhaps, to alter how they allocate headquarters costs. It may not only take time, it may take some courage to watch this happen, but it is a must.

We'll talk about this later in Chapter 4.

So, remember, the only good reason to open a branch office is because you expect that office will generate profit per shareholder equal or greater than the profit per shareholder of the rest of the company, on a medium-term basis. Unless, of course, you insist on opening a new branch for one of the bad reasons.

Chapter 2 – Ok, Where?

Of course, the first big question is *where* do we open a branch office? That's what everyone wants to study first, right? Or, is it really the first question? Or, how do we figure out where to open our next or first branch office?

I think, actually, that it doesn't matter one iota where you open an office, if you do the other things right it should be successful. What really does matter is not *where* to locate but *who* will run it and how it's organized and incentivized. Wherever the new office is located, there will be stiff competition so be prepared for a lot of losing.

But, let's take a look at how you might decide *where* to locate a new office.

Work. The biggest and perhaps only reason to locate to a certain area is that the area has work that you do **and** the clients there prefer to give the work to local companies. Some areas have a lot of work. The area is growing and there is a lot of government as well as private sector work similar to the work that you do. We are all aware of the "hot" places around the world. Texas, for example, always seems to be growing and has lots of work. Alternately, the "rust belt" has lots of local firms but dwindling resources to fund projects.

However, even areas that aren't growing and prospering have some work. Many times, it may be government mandated work. Or, work from a local private sector company that may be booming. Some years ago, it was safe to say that North Dakota was not a boom area. But, then the discovery of the Parshall Oil Field in 2006, caused huge growth there. That growth meant growth in housing, infrastructure, light manufacturing and all sorts of related industries, not to mention the oil business itself. But, with the declining oil prices beginning in 2015, the boom slowed.

In this way, many areas decline or flourish with changes in the local economy, markets and mandates. If your headquarters is in an area that is declining, it may be wise to be looking to open branches in areas that are flourishing.

Government mandates may include new air quality regulations causing a lot of air quality controls to be installed; or, clean water regulations; or, hazardous waste clean-up sites.

Private companies can suddenly grow as their services or products become hot and they may need your services to expand. Again, a good example is the oil business with changing regulations and changing oil prices, private sector companies that thrive with higher oil prices are likely to boom or bust based on those prices. So, it partly depends on the work that your firm does. You know the hot areas for your businesses better than anyone.

The same may be true with industries such as solar power, the coal industry, the steel production industry and many other such manufacturers and producers.

Brilliant Advise Box

The more work there is in an area, the more firms will show up to do it. Planning on opening a branch in a hot market area does not necessarily mean you are apt to get a lot of work there.

However, as localities have more and more new work, more and more competitors will show up to compete against you.
And, in areas where it is not booming, there are hungry competitors languishing there and wanting you to go away.

When you are doing your business plan for the new office, investigate and evaluate the present and future work in the targeted geographic area.

Go to the area and meet with clients and customers and ask questions:
1. Who has work (that you do) in the locality now and expected in the future? How much work? If it is a government agency, the amount of work coming up will be a matter of record. Airport authorities, sewer districts, water districts, transportation districts, etc., have long-term plans that call for spending that can be a source of information for your evaluation. It is somewhat trickier to obtain information from private sector clients, but they may offer information if you ask the right people.
2. Find out from the clients that are in your proposed new location, how they select firms to do work for them. Does that fit your culture and your business plan?
3. What firms are doing the work for the entities that have work coming up? Are they firms with strong local presence? Is there a lot of competition?
4. And, find out if you can, whether your firm can get work if they don't have a local presence. Some local entities may say, "sure" and others may say, "no way" but you need to ask.
5. While you're in town pounding the pavement, and taking folks to lunch, be on the look-out for some key hires for the new branch office. You may find a candidate to open and run your new branch office or someone to lead one of your practice areas there.

Reputation. Speaking of work, a huge part of your ability to get work is the reputation of your firm as well as you, personally. Remember, clients hire firms that they trust and they have to know you before they can trust you. The further away the branch is located from the headquarters, the firm's reputation will be less recognized and you will be less trusted. Some firms follow the "strawberry plant" philosophy. Strawberry plants send shoots and grow new plants close to the mother plant. In this way, the firm will be better known and have a stronger reputation near its historic geographic areas of influence.

For example, a firm that may be headquartered and have historic influence in Orlando, will likely have a strong reputation in Tampa, Fort Myers, Gainesville and Jacksonville. However, there may be little or no name recognition for the firm in San Francisco, Seattle, Salt Lake City and Houston. You need to have a strong reason to venture too far from home. (Prestige is not a strong reason.)

> **Brilliant Advise Box**
>
> Your new branch office will likely be more successful if you locate it where you have a positive reputation. Don't venture so far from home that no one has heard of you. Instead, take a look at major cities in your region where you have a reputation that you can build on.

So, take a look at the major metro areas not too far from your HQs. Maybe you have a client or two in some of them. Maybe you already have a reputation in a few of them. The nice thing is that you haven't messed up any work in those other places so your reputation is likely to be good. By the way, that gives you a leg up on your competition in the new area. Your competition has likely screwed up some work in your new area where as you have not, which might be a nice advantage once you open.

Your primary places to consider are those cities where you are going to have name recognition by many clients there but that you are far enough away that you're not going to get work there without a local office.

Remember, you will only get work from clients that trust you and they can't trust you unless they know you. However, this can be offset by hiring a local person that they do know and trust. We'll talk about that in Chapter 3.

Market Research. I know of a firm who wanted to open a new branch office but didn't have a location in mind. The firm's principals, however, each had opinions, mostly based on their market areas. The firm spent thousands of hours and thousands of dollars on consultants to obtain data on twelve different cities. Data included information on public and private work, growth, availability of staff, strength of competition and expectations for future work. Market research was commissioned to try to evaluate future work in that area for the various market areas of the firm. All of this data was massaged and sorted and analyzed and summarized. The list was then culled from twelve to six locations.

"Recon teams" were then sent out to those 6 locations at excessive cost and meetings were held with potential clients in each area. Data were further refined and analyzed to determine realistic expectations of work in each of those cities. For each of the six locations, potential office managers were considered. Would the firm send someone there to open an office or hire someone who is already there and who knows the territory. (More on that in Chapter 3).

The list of six was then shortlisted to three locations. A presentation was then made to the board detailing all of the findings of the study. Casual comments by firm principals were made and accepted. Opinions were voiced and further refinements made. Finally, the vice president of marketing announced that the winning location just happened to be his hometown and, indeed, he was going to go there himself and open the new branch there. And, in fact, he announced that he was going to move there and run it. It was predestined that he would choose this place although no one realized it until it was too late. The data was manipulated, positive reasons to open an office there were emphasized and negative reasons were ignored.

The VP of Marketing did, indeed, move to this location and did open an office there and ran it successfully until he retired. The office is still there and is still successful.

> **Brilliant Advise Box**
>
> Market research isn't going to tell you too much. You'll mostly find out what you already know. Do your own market research by getting a subscription to Sorkin's or some other similar publication.

So, I believe that it doesn't matter too much *where* you locate, it matters more *how* you open an office and *who* you choose to run it.

With that in mind, my thoughts on how to evaluate where to open an office are:
1. Think about *who* in your present organization might be a great office manager. (See Chapter 3). Where would be a great location for that person? Maybe you have a great, loyal person who is ready for promotion and who knows your organization and who has developed friendships among many in your organization. This person is ready for the next step but you don't have a place for them. Take a look at where they are from originally. Where do their parents live? Where is their spouse from? Where do the grandparents live? What other history does this person have in

certain locations? Where did the person go to college? What places will match the culture of your person.
2. Consider the balance of work to competitors. Realize that places that are growing with a lot of potential work for your firm, already has substantial competition for your firm. It will probably take a lot of money and time and marketing savvy to get work there. Alternately, places that are not growing a lot have less work but also have less competition. There will be battles for new work in these locations among competitors who have been in town for a while, so, again, your firm will have substantial competition for any work that emerges.
3. The success of your next branch office is tied mostly with:
    a. Who you choose to run it.
    b. The incentives and financial arrangements of your new office.
    c. The skills of the staff that you hire and/or relocate.
    d. The marketing ability of your firm and your new office manager.
    e. And, not where it is.

International Offices. The trials and tribulations of starting a new office in an international location are astronomical. There are so many issues regarding taxes, finances, laws, security, corruption, terrorism, religion and culture that they are far too many to discuss. Maybe I'll write a new book to just cover that.

If you are targeting an international location for a new office, you might consider that most firms open a "sales" office instead of a working office. The sales office will likely have a local person in charge who knows the culture, the way companies hire firms, the competition and the local way of doing taxes, finances, laws, security, corruption, etc. The local office manager will likely be from that country and will likely know very little about your company or your culture.

I know a firm who had a branch office – really a sales office – in Taipei. They had a local Taiwanese guy run it. He was a "loose cannon". He went after work that the firm didn't do. He made promises to potential clients that the firm couldn't keep. He spent a lot of money on expensive dinners and entertainment that never amounted to any work. But, again, the office was not set up as a profit center so that the costs of the office were melded into the practice division and no one really ever knew how much it all cost.

Some firms buy a local firm giving them an instantly complete office with local workers and local managers. Or, they may buy controlling interest in a local firm. But, this too is a treacherous route with lots of pitfalls, loopholes and risk. You better expect huge profits to offset the huge costs of an international office. You will have to overcome major cultural differences and tap-dance through a plethora of local laws as well as US laws. I hope you have a lot of money set aside for international law firm fees.

> **Brilliant Advise Box**
>
> If you are not interested in losing a lot of money or, you are not a large, sophisticated firm, consider staying away from international offices. Of course, there are exceptions, but avoid that mess if you can.

Enough of that. Proceed at your own risk.

As I said earlier, it's more important to talk about *who* to open a new office so let's amble ably to the next chapter.

Chapter 3 -- Who?

So now that you've picked a location for a new office, what's next? You may already have an office manager in mind or you may not. In fact, if you take my advice, you will choose an office manager and *then* choose a place based on the background and talents of your chosen office manager. You may already have one or more clients in the location which may influence your next steps.

However, it's my way of thinking that your next step ought to be to find someone to open it and run it. That person will be instrumental in looking at real estate, selecting the "right" part of town for the office, for hiring and firing people and, of course, for doing much of the marketing in the new location. They will also be coordinating all sorts of important things with the folks back at HQ.

The big question is this: Do you relocate a loyal member of your firm from headquarters to open the new office? Or, do you hire a new person off the street who is already there? There are pros and cons to each that we need to explore.

> **Brilliant Advice Box**
>
> The very best way to choose a branch manager is to hire several people from the big university in the targeted city. Bring the new, entry-level people to HQ and let them work there for a five- to ten-year period while you give them some diverse training in a lot of your company areas. Then, choose one or more to send back to the city to start an office or to populate an existing office. In this way, you get someone who is from that city and who wants to go "home" and still knows your firm and its culture.

Relocating a Person from Your Firm
This person who you might relocate knows your firm and has dozens of important relationships with people in your

headquarters. This person knows the culture of your firm which is, of itself, extremely important.

If you have other branch offices, the person likely has relationships with some of those office managers who can be great resources as well. This person from headquarters knows the culture of your firm and will likely transfer that culture to the new location. They, hopefully, know the firm's financial condition and is knowledgeable about the profit and loss centers of the firm. They also know the market areas of the company and many of the company experts in the various service areas of your firm.

This person has tremendous knowledge of your firm and this knowledge will be extremely valuable in the coming years. This person will be the firm's eyes and ears in the new location and it is very important that the person be loyal and dedicated to the success of the new office.

Some companies, when relocating a member of their firm to run the office, make sure that the new office manager knows that it is a "one way ticket". It is unlikely that the person will ever return to headquarters. They are there for the "duration", to sink or swim, and to retire in the new location. This gives the person some reverse "incentive" to succeed.

Although I'm not a big fan of reverse or negative incentives, I like a lot the explorer Hernán Cortés who scuttled his ships after he landed in what is now Veracruz, Mexico to discourage his folks from wanting to retreat and sail home.

There are many considerations when choosing someone from your firm to be the new office manager. First, this person must be replaceable in the headquarters. Their work in the new office will be full-time-plus, so the person needs to be replaced back in the HQ, which may cause further concern.

Second, moving to a new city can be a difficult thing, especially for a senior, well-respected member of your firm. This person will likely have relationships with existing clients that your firm does not want to jeopardize. However, it is unlikely that person will be able to carry these clients or projects to the new location.

This person may be married and their spouse may have a high-paying job that they don't want to give up. And, of course, the kids are probably in school and the person's family will be giving up their church, their doctors, their house, their neighborhood, their neighbors and, somewhat, their friends.

So, the firm needs to do some things to make it as easy as possible so that your new manager can completely focus on their new responsibility. This includes, of course, a promotion, a raise and an increased bonus. If your firm normally uses non-compete agreements, this would be an appropriate time to have this person sign one if they haven't already, assuming they are binding in the state where the person is moving. (If non-compete agreements are binding in your state and you don't have them in place, I recommend that you do so right away.)

It might be nice to help this person sell their house and to include moving expenses and a generous program to reimburse them for their many trips back and forth during the transition period. You want your new office manager to be focused on the new office.

However, there is a downside to this approach. This person who you plan to move, indeed knows your company and understands the markets of the firm, but the person may not necessarily have knowledge of the new location. The person will be opening an office and facing many internal challenges as well as hiring new people for the office. But, the biggest challenge will be developing relationships with prospective clients in the new area. It often takes years to develop those relationships as well as years to get work from a new client.

Even if the new office manager is originally from this location, they have likely not kept up with the goings-on there nor the politics and local atmosphere. Many of the past potential clients are gone and others have taken their place.

A nice balance to this approach is for the new office manager who is relocating from HQ, to hire a senior local person who knows the new location, many of the potential clients there and many potential new employees. This second, senior local person can also bring respect and trust to the new firm. Don't forget, clients hire firms based on the trust that they have for the firm and there may be little knowledge or trust of the firm or the new office manager.

> **Brilliant Advise Box**
>
> A nice balance is an office manager who is relocated from the headquarters coupled with a senior person hired from the targeted location. But, be careful of doing the reverse.

If a senior, locally well-known person joins your firm and becomes a "partner" with the new office manager, you now have all of the bases covered: knowledge of the firm, relationships within the firm, knowledge of the local area and clients and, most importantly, some trust with the new office because of the senior local person.

Of course, it's not always easy to find this senior person and if you do, they will likely cost a premium. So, the downside of this approach is that you now have two senior people (and perhaps others) in the new office with very little billable work to do unless HQ can send some work to them. More on that in Chapter 5.

Hiring a Local Office Manager
It is obvious that the opposite is true if you hire a local person to start and run your new branch office. Theoretically, that person knows the local decision makers and many local clients. But, often, they may only know potential clients within their historic service area.

For example, if you have selected a local transportation engineer to run your new office the person will likely know the people in the area who choose firms to do transportation work. But, that person may not know the local folks in the wastewater business or the storm water business or the chemical processing business or the hospital construction business and, yet, that person may be asked to be the "front guy" for those clients as well.

And, of course, this person likely knows very little about the culture and inner-workings of your firm. They have a huge learning curve in how the firm works when it comes to HR, fiscal planning and reporting, marketing and sales, etc. And, they undoubtedly have few contacts inside of the firm and scant information as to the many service areas of the firm and who the experts are in each of them. This person is going to need a *lot* of help as well as a *lot* of trips back to HQ taking up time that could be spent calling on potential clients and actually doing some work.

How are you going to help them? How much time are you willing to give? Instead of Moses going to the mountain, consider sending the Mountain to Moses. Send some of your staff to help the new person. For example, send your QC Manager and/or your specifications manager and or your marketing VP, etc. Although their time is valuable too, they can afford to give the new manager a little of their time and save his travel time back to HQ – just saying.

Similarly, to the first method, you can balance the inadequacies of the second method by relocating a senior person to the new place. In order to help the new office manager, relocate a person who knows the firm and its culture and its market areas and some of its experts and maybe even has a knowledge of the new location because he grew up there or went to college there or, whatever.

I have seen firms do it both ways. And, for sure, I have seen successes and failures with both methods. It depends on the person, as you already know.

Are you willing to send your best and brightest person off to a new location with a one-way ticket? Are you willing to spend the money to let it happen?

There is a third way – sort of method 1b.

Moving from another branch office.
Another option that I've seen done is to move a bright young prospect from one branch office to start a new one. Often, you may have a great person stuck in a branch office somewhere with essentially no upward mobility. Consider moving that person to your newly picked location. In this case, you have a hybrid situation. The person knows your firm and your firm culture as well as has knowledge of branch office supporters back at the HQ. The person may or may not have knowledge of the new location but may have reasons to want to go there. The best reason, of course, is that the person now has an opportunity to "go

forth and do good" and make a name in your firm as well as be the boss in the new office.

As with the other methods, there are drawbacks. It may be harmful to the existing branch to yank this person from their current branch leaving a void in leadership, expertise or marketing savvy. But, remember that it may be incentive for anyone in a branch office in your firm to know that opportunities exist for them to enhance their career and climb the corporate ladder.

And, the Best Way is to Grow your Own and Replant. What do I mean by that? I know a person who grew up in and graduated from college in Phoenix. Upon graduation, he was hired by a professional services firm headquartered in Dallas where he moved and started his career. The firm did not have an office in Phoenix but wanted one in the future. The new employee was one of several who were from Phoenix and who came to work in Dallas. Over the next few years, each of those people were moved around different parts of the company, learning different areas of their practice. Each of those young people gradually started to "settle down" and got married and started having kids and by golly, each was interested in moving back to Phoenix where their parents were and where their real "home" was.

By then, the firm had an office in Phoenix that was growing and the timing was perfect to send these young people back home. They brought with them the culture of the firm, knowledge of specialized people back in the HQ and in-depth awareness of the firm's practices and service areas.

All were glad to be sent home. One of them became the new branch manager a few years after getting back to Phoenix. This was a huge success story but one that is difficult to replicate unless you are bold, committed and lucky.

I knew a guy with a competing company that was a great leader and a great marketer and a great manager. He was a vice president in his firm, headquartered in Chicago, and was squarely in line for even greater things. One day, the CEO approached him and asked him to relocate to Seattle to take over their branch office there which was in trouble. The CEO had just fired the branch manager and went to his best guy to go out there and straighten it out.

So, he did. But, he did not relocate to Seattle. His wife and kids stayed behind in Chicago because they had no interest in leaving their schools or jobs or friends. Each set of grandparents lived near them. So, the VP travelled from Chicago to Seattle every Sunday night and flew home on Friday nights – for over a year. Ugh. He did is best and managed to turn the office around. He then went to the CEO and requested that he be given his old job back in HQ. He had found a replacement for himself in Seattle and the long commute was not only hard on him but extremely hard on his wife and children who were without a dad all week.

Much to the VP's surprise, the CEO said "no". The VP was told that the company needed him in Seattle and that he had to choose between Seattle or resigning. Ouch. The ships had been burned and he didn't even know it.

He did not move to Seattle but instead chose to resign and landed a nice job with a company in Chicago. As a result, the firm was out a great person on a fast-track and the VP essentially wasted his many years with the firm.

Be careful when you burn the ships.

Chapter 4 – Goals and objectives of a branch office

One of the first steps you will need to take with your newly selected branch manager – even if there is no branch yet – is to lay out the mission of this new endeavor. So, what is the mission of your new branch? What are you trying to do? Although this question is fundamental, we often fail to ask ourselves this question and many firm principals charge ahead without even knowing where they are trying to go.

It's also a pretty good idea to make sure your newly selected branch office manager knows pretty well what the goals and objectives are – and what they are not.

So, let's give some thought to what you are trying to accomplish. There are a lot of legitimate objectives to opening a new office and there are some objectives, sometimes surprisingly embraced by firms, that are not legitimate. Let's take a look.

Objective number 1 – increase firm profit per shareholder. Remember this reason from Chapter 1? It is the one fundamental objective for opening any new office. But, what does that really mean?

Hopefully, your firm has a detailed accounting system that incorporates a number of profit centers as well as corporate allocations of overheads to each of those profit centers. The cost of the CEO and the CEO's staff, who are seldom billable, are allocated to each profit center on some basis. Of course, other corporate overheads, such as the accounting department, the HR department, the corporate marketing department, etc. are also allocated to the profit centers.

The allocation might be based on number of full-time equivalents in each profit center, or that month's revenue in each profit center, or, your monthly revenue or, however your board wants to allocate them.

However, it is important to scrutinize corporate overheads and correctly allocate them. For example, the cost of the CEO and CFO and their staffs are justifiably allocable equally to each profit center. But, the cost of a new roof at HQ is not. The new roof should be allocated to the profit centers at that location. Corporate marketing brochures should be allocated to all profit centers; but, marketing materials produced for a specific market area for a specific profit center should be allocated to just that profit center.

If you don't have the right accounting codes and allocation policy set up, the CFO needs to set them up. And, someone under the CFO has to monitor expenses as they come in to make sure they are properly coded. Fair is fair.

I know a firm headquartered in Pittsburgh who bought season tickets to the Pirates in order to take clients and/or bigwigs to the ballgame. The substantial cost of those tickets was allocated as *corporate overhead* to HQ as well as each branch office and other profit center as a corporate marketing expense. But, in reality, those tickets only benefited those at HQ. Branches rarely had someone that wanted to go to a Pirates game.

Meanwhile, if a branch office bought season tickets to their local ball club, those costs were charged to the branch office. In that way, the branch office was charged 100% for their own tickets plus got to pay for their "share" of the Pirates tix. That's a tough battle to win. If it were just MLB tickets, that might be ok, but it's a lot more than that.

There are tons of headquarters' expenses that get charged to corporate overhead that shouldn't be.

Similarly, one of my branch office manager friends with another company, got their share of the company picnic allocated to their office as well as the cost of their own picnic. No fair.

If all you are talking about is baseball tickets or picnics, then we don't have a big problem, but the philosophy is important and the policy has to be established to make expenses properly allocated.

Otherwise, your branch offices will find it more and more difficult to show a profit. It's hard enough without burdening them with costs that do not benefit them.

This brings us to the major point of this book but one that may be overlooked by many firms: each branch office needs to be a separate profit center with appropriately allocated expenses and revenues. Gee, I think I've said that before and I hope that it has sunk in.

Don't make the mistake of hiding the costs of any branch office, especially a new one, by not making it a proper profit center on day one.

Do we need to talk more about that or have I said it enough?

And, who needs to know about the profit situation of your profit centers? The profit center managers, of course, including each branch manager. And, the shareholders and principals of your firm. Some firms share financial information of their firm with all of their employees. Do you?

Objective number 2 – sell more work. It's pretty obvious that in order to make profit, you have to sell profitable work. Have you thought through how you're going to sell more work? Just being somewhere, as you well know, doesn't assure that you'll sell work there. Someone has to go out and pound the pavement, write qualification packages, develop proposals and make presentations, that is, if you're lucky and smart enough to get shortlisted.

Branch offices have a terrible Chicken and Egg Syndrome. It's real hard to sell work if you don't have people but you can't hire people until you sell work.

But, let's skip the rest of this and talk about marketing in Chapter 6. Instead, I want to talk about *doing* the work. Many firm principals are enticed to open new branch offices by imagining that work will be sold in the new location and brought or sent back to the HQ and done there. The new location, so the thinking goes, will send profitable work back to the home office where all of the experts are and where the folks are great at doing the work efficiently and with superior quality.

That's how it often goes. I know of a firm who had a branch office in Mobile. One of the many mistakes it made was to not have the office be a profit center. Rather, when opened, it became part of the overall profit center of a division in their home office in Atlanta. No one ever knew whether the office made profit or not as the office's billable time and sales were all melded into the much bigger division back in HQ.

> **Brilliant Advise Box**
>
> Good hunters like to hunt, kill, skin, cook and eat their own game – not take someone's roadkill.

When the Mobile office managed to sell some profitable work, their home division naturally thought that they, in

Atlanta, could do the work much more efficiently and with higher quality so they would "take" the work and do it there. Meanwhile, in order to keep the Mobile office billable, they would send them their crappy work to do, often at a much lower profitability. It was a no-win situation for the good folks in Mobile.

The good folks in Mobile soon got tired of this game and the good employees quit and went to work somewhere that they could have meaningful work to do. Good hunters like to hunt, kill, skin, cook and eat their own game – not take someone else's roadkill. If you play this game with your new people in your office, don't expect them to stick around for long. Instead, any mediocre people that you might hire will stick and you will end up with a mediocre office content with roadkill, no profits and lack of respect. Of course, the next step is closing the office. I've seen it happen too many times.

So, Objective Number 2 has to be re-written. Sell work for the new office to do and to build-on.

Objective Number 2b – sell work to new clients. Remember that one of the top reasons to open a new office is to sell work to clients who only hire firms with a local presence. If your new office is just doing work for an existing client – one that was already hiring you, you haven't accomplished anything except to make doing their work less efficient. If that's the case, your firm was doing their work more profitably and with more experienced people before you opened the branch office, so your new office hasn't accomplished what it was set out to do.

Besides making money, the next big objective is to sell and do work for *new* clients that heretofore would not hire you unless you had a significant local presence. So, let's list that as an objective of our new office. This means that your new office will have to market to new clients. How are you going to do that? Are you offering new services to those clients?

Branch offices only exist to sell work to clients who want their work done locally. BO's should sell *all* of the work that your firm does, to clients in their geographic area. Alternately, your practice groups back at HQ try to sell work that their practice does to targeted clients world-wide. Branch offices' main objective is to develop relationships and *trust* (there's that word again) with new, local clients. Then, when that local client needs work done, the local BO will lead it and do it with the appropriate amount of help from the appropriate practice area guru's.

> **Brilliant Advise Box**
>
> Your new branch office needs to focus on selling work to new clients and to make that a goal. Find a way to measure that and report it. Selling work to clients for whom you've been working for 10 years doesn't accomplish anything that you want.

More on that in Chapter 5. For now, let's just list it and go on.

Objective number 3 – grow the office. Let's presume that you want this office to become a self-sufficient office, hunting, cleaning, cooking and eating its kills. Of course, HQ will lend a hand and provide expertise and counsel and culture enrichment. But, for the most part, we want the office to grow and add good people and increase staff and capabilities of the firm at large, all while making lots of profit, right? I hope so.

Hiring good, talented people is one of the hardest objectives of a new office. Like any team, it takes time to build a group of people who know how to work together and follow the leader and respect each other's skills and come together to win the Super Bowl or the World Series or the World Cup or the Stanley Cup.

In order to hire talented people who can start and lead and grow a new practice in your new office, you have to recruit them and you will have to pay them handsomely to change jobs. These folks nearly always are working somewhere else and are, generally, happy. So, you as a firm will have to bite the bullet and seek out people who will make a difference and pay them to switch to this fledgling office and to this new firm that they know little about. Alternately, it's also a good idea to send talented folks from HQ or another branch, to lead a group in the new office. Of course, when you do this, you leave a vacant position that most likely will need to be filled, and, again, you have to pay for the person to move and settle in at the new location.

In general, I think it's a great plan to do a combination of hiring locally and sending some folks from HQ out to the hinterlands at the new location. In this way, you end up with people in your new branch who know the culture and clients of the new location as well as folks who know the culture and expertise and service areas of the firm.

Objective number 4 – hire great people. It's hard to make a nice profit right away and it's hard to sell profitable work right away and it's also hard to hire great people right away. Let's see, let's make a list of things that great people want in order to come to work for a new company (I'm pretty big on lists):

> **Brilliant Advise Box**
>
> Infuse your new branch office with talented people from the HQ. These people, ideally, have some connections to the location of your new branch. They bring to your new office the culture and history and knowledge of the company. I think that you ought to shoot for relocating around 20 percent of your new office's staff from HQ, or another branch.

a. More money. Most "great" people will need to make more money working for you than working where they are now. Are you willing? Even if it skews your pay scale? Does your firm's salary structure take into account differences in cost-of-living at various locations in the US? Do you have knowledge of the salaries paid to great people in the location where you are targeting?
b. Incentive. Great people, by their very nature, want to have incentive to make more money as well as get promotions based on their performance. Does your firm provide incentives in the form of bonuses or promotions or, whatever? If not, are you ready to hire the great people that you are going to need?
c. Technical growth. Most great people want to practice their profession and to continue to get bigger and better at what they want to do. Engineers want to continue to do more complex and more highly technical engineering. Architects want to work on bigger and more interesting buildings. Lawyers want bigger and more interesting cases. Are you prepared to let this happen?
d. Opportunities. Great people want to work on interesting projects or cases regardless of where they are located. Will your firm's culture allow the great people that get hired in your new branch to work on projects located elsewhere in your firm?

I had a great employee at one point in my career who was a mechanical engineer and who wanted to do process mechanical engineering. He was a leader in our branch office and had a following of clients in our area. But, most of the work that he ended up leading or managing was pretty simple

HVAC mechanical or industrial work. Why? Because the process practice in our firm was not interested in letting him be a part of the complex, interesting process engineering work that they did. Much to my dismay, he quit. We didn't have a way to incentivize the process practice to encourage them to use his talents. After he left and never did ever find what he was looking for, we started to do more and more interesting process engineering and ironically, he ended up becoming our client at one point.

It's easy to get caught up worrying about sales and profit and quality control and growth and how corporate overheads are allocated, but good branch managers will understand that you have to take care of your good people. One of the ways to do that is to make sure that they are technically fulfilled.

Objective number 5 – develop a new, niche service area. Whoa – what? I think it's a great objective for the new office to eventually develop a new service area that the firm has not done or is not noted for. This is a great opportunity in a new location, when you're hiring new, great people, to pick up someone who has some specialized expertise that he/she can develop into a new, niche service area. This is a great way to grow the office while offering those services nationally. Undoubtedly, this takes a while to accomplish but, if you think this is a good idea, let's put it on our list as a mid-term goal with a lower priority.

Above, we talked about opportunity and incentive. Is your firm willing to hire a great person in your new location and then let that person grow a new practice in a niche market?

Objective number 6 – do quality work. Oh – let's not forget about that. How will you promote and monitor their work? Let's talk about that in Chapter 9.

That's probably enough for now. We can add others later, but those are the big one's right? - profit, sales, growth and quality.

> **Brilliant Advise Box**
>
> It's a great objective for the new office to eventually develop a new service area that the firm has not done or is not noted for.

So, now we have a start on the goals and objectives of the new branch office. There are a couple of things we need to do to tag along to those goals: 1) make sure the entire board of directors or principal group is in agreement on them; and, 2) that they are communicated clearly to the new office manager.

That's pretty simple – but it's a big, important step that won't be as easy as you think.

So, if we want your Board of Directors and the principal group to buy-in, then you need to communicate your objectives to them. I suggest you develop a Business Plan for the new office. Better yet – have the new office manager-elect do it. Have that person present it to the Board and then, once the Board blesses it, you're off and running.

> **Brilliant Advise Box**
>
> Before you go off opening a new branch office, have the new branch office manager-designate, develop a Business Plan for the office covering the first three years.

What should be in this Business Plan? Hopefully, you already know how to develop and write a company business plan. But, your new BOM may not so he or she may need a little nudging and coaching in the right direction.

Here's my outline for a Branch Office Business Plan:

1. Executive Summary
2. Goals and Objectives of the new Branch Office
    a. Sales goals for each of the first three years
    b. Growth goals for each of the first three years
    c. Billable time goals, assuming you normally measure that.
    d. Effective Labor Multiplier and Break-even multiplier goals for the first three years
    e. Profit goals for the first three years.
3. Potential and Existing Clients in the New Location
    a. A list including the type of work they normally outsource.
    b. Who does work for them now and their selection process if known.
    c. Estimated volume of work for each during the next three years.
4. Competition in the New Location
    The firms that you normally compete with within each of your firm's practice area that are active in the new location.
5. Doing work and Project Management
6. Quality Control and Risk Management in the New Location.
7. Sales Plan in the New Location
    a. How you are going to get new clients to trust your firm?
    b. Number of new clients vs. existing clients.
8. Probable Location of the New Branch in the Region.
9. Sensitivity Analysis of the Plan
    How sensitive are the profit goals to less-than-plan sales, billable time, overhead costs?

You can add a lot of other things if you wish. It will be hard enough to pull all of this together. Maybe your firm has a template for developing a business plan for a new branch office. I hope so. If not, start with this one.

It will be interesting to look back on your plan after the first three years – if your office is still around. Did you manage to get work with some of the new clients listed? How did your billable time and revenue projections compare with actuals?

Most important, how did your profitability projections compare with your actual profit. No doubt, your actual experience will be substantially different than projected, but I think it's a great way for a new branch manager to understand what it's going to take to operate the new branch at a profit.

Chapter 5 – Doing Work

Ok, so now we have some introductory thoughts on paper and we have started to work on Objective No. 2 – Selling work, and by golly, the new location is starting to get work to do. Now what?

I believe that there are several fundamental truths that sometimes conflict with one another; in fact, there are at least five.

Fundamental Truth No. 1 (here we go again): Clients expect work to be done by people experienced in the scope of work of the project. True? If you were a client, you hired this new, local firm to do some work for you trusting that they know what they're doing and that they will put qualified, experienced people on it. Indeed, there were probably resumes in the firm's proposal to the client showing resumes of experienced people and the client trusted that those people will work on their project.

But, some of those people are often not located in the new branch office. The firm's best, most experienced people are elsewhere: either back at HQ or in another branch office. So, the conflict is that clients expect your firm's best, experienced people to work on their project but your less experienced people need work to do in your new location. If you put the new branch people on the job, you are not giving the client your best.

So, one solution is to put your people on the project and get your firm's most experienced people to watch over their work and, perhaps, teach them how to do the work. But, oh, that can be a problem. Even with technology that allows for instant access to drawings and tables and work products, most experienced people do not have the patience to train new people to do what they already know how to do, especially in a new branch office.

Yet, this is exactly what you will normally have to do. When a new branch office sells work, they want to do it. Yes, they may need help and oversight and guidance. But, let them do it. This may not always be the case but – now think about it – if you are in a new branch office, trying desperately to develop relationships and sell some work for your people to do, and you finally succeed, what will happen if you send that work off to others in the HQ to do? Your good people will quit and your new client will likely balk at having their work done back at HQ or in your distant LA Office or wherever, by people they don't know.

I know a firm that had a branch office that specialized in transportation design services. The firm did water treatment design very well but only back at HQ. The branch spent lots of time and money building relationships with one of the nearby cities and eventually were asked to do a small water treatment study for them. The local branch immediately called the lead water treatment person back at HQ who then immediately "took over". The headquarters guy called the client, set up a meeting and basically, left the new branch altogether out of the meeting and the project. This, of course, upset all of the branch staff as well as the client. It took many months to recover.

Fundamental Truth No. 2: The HQ will (almost) always be able to do work more efficiently than the new branch office. The HQ has been working together for decades – maybe over a century. They are a well-oiled machine. The HQ has talented people who know how to knock out a project efficiently, quickly and profitably. If they didn't the firm wouldn't still be in business.

The new branch office is composed of people who are not used to working together. Some of their people aren't the best at their job and there are likely a number of technical holes that need filling. The new branch may get lucky and finish the job and make the client happy and make some profit, but it is definitely a fundamental truth that the HQ can do the work better.

But, the conflict is that if you want a new branch office that can sell work and do work profitably, you have to let them do their thing. They need time to get to know each other, to understand who is good in their new org and who isn't and how to get more efficient.

When I was a kid, they used to have the football "College All-Star Football Classic" in late summer every year. This game would match the best college seniors from the previous season against the NFL champion team – the Super Bowl Champion in later years.

I remember my dad and I always watching that game and always rooting for the underdog college all-stars. The game was played from 1937 through 1976. During the 26-year span of 1951 through 1976, the college all-stars won in 1955, 1958 and 1963 – three times in 26 years. How can you possibly expect a group of men who have not worked together before and who don't know each other's strengths and weaknesses to beat the super bowl champion? You can't expect it and, for sure, you can't expect your new branch office to do work more efficiently than your HQ even though they might get lucky 3 times out of every 26 tries.

So, have some patience and understand this fundamental truth. CEO's can try to help but by sending some folks to the BO but that's going to cost some cash as well.

Fundamental Truth No. 3: - your new branch office will never do work with as high a quality as the HQ. No matter how hard you try and no matter how much effort your QC people put into making your new branch office a QC Machine, like Fundamental Truth No. 2, they will never be as good as HQ. Of course, again, there are going to be exceptions. Your new, bright, great employees that you hire in the new branch, will do good work and sometimes, even better than their counterparts back at HQ, but rarely.

So, you are going to have to accept that it will take years of effort and heartache and, perhaps, some liability claims and mad clients for the new branch to get up to the level of the HQ. I want you to try but it will be an expensive investment. Fundamental Truth 3b is that the more quality control you employ, the less profit you will realize in the short term. Right? Every hour you spend checking and re-checking work is an hour's worth of profit you don't realize. The exception is that when your QC program finds mistakes that would have cost beaucoup dollars in claims down the road.

Again, you have to let the branch office do the work that they sell and help them to do it with quality but it may be a rough road for a while.

The conflict is that most CEO's and COO's and QC managers are risk averse. It's their big thing. Risk management and all of that. If you are risk averse, you have no business encouraging a new branch office. You can have a new sales office, perhaps, and try to sell work and send it all back to the QC Machine to do at HQ but, as we know, that won't really work either.

If you want a new branch office to sell work and do work profitably, you are going to have to squint, squirm, dig deep and accept the fact that they will not do the best work in your firm – at least at first. You might get to know your insurance carriers pretty well.

Fundamental Truth No. 4 – your new branch office will not be as profitable as your HQ for a long time. I assume that you already know this truth by now. Remember, that the main reason that you are setting up the branch office is to make more profit per shareholder. But, it's not going to happen for a while – maybe a long while.

There are exceptions. I know a firm who opened an office in the upper mid-west and they were smart enough to hire a new, great person who had a good client following and a new niche market. Suddenly, one of the new person's clients called and started giving highly profitable work to the new office. The new office, through the new, great guy, managed to hire some talented staff to do the new work and the office was embarrassingly profitable. They dug for water and discovered gold.

> **Brilliant Advise Box**
>
> Your branch offices will take a long time to match the profitability of your HQ office or practice divisions. Be patient but understand this fundamental truth.

The new office grew and grew and did more and more of this highly profitable work and did it with quality. The office was so profitable that they invested in other great people to start other practices but it wasn't as easy as it seemed. Eventually, the great client with the great, new profitable work dried up and the office was left with a lot of talented people and no work. But, for a while, like about 10 years, it looked great. So, great that the office manager got a huge bonuses and eventually a huge promotion out of it. But the other practices that they tried to start had a much rockier road, as should be expected.

The conflict should be evident. The only really good reason to open a new branch office is to make more profit per shareholder. Your new branch office is not likely to do that for a long while – unless you dig for water and strike gold.

So, what is the answer? What is the Fundamental Truth about doing work in a branch office? Is there a secret?

The best way to do work in a branch office is by doing it as a combined team. Your project team should consist, mostly, of people in the branch office but should include talented people from HQ or another branch who are willing to do some traveling and help out the new kids.

> **Brilliant Advise Box**
>
> The best way to do work in a branch office is by doing it as a combined team of folks from the branch and from the HQ practice areas and, perhaps, from some other branch offices.

In order to make this happen, it takes a lot of management effort. It takes recognizing those in the HQ who go the extra mile with a bonus or a strong pat on the back. It takes management emphasis. It takes removal of silo's and walls that you, actually, have erected. See Fundamental Truth No. 5 – next.

Fundamental Truth No. 5 – you have to remove barriers erected that prevent what you want to happen. You have an accounting system in your firm that tracks and measures financial success against goals. The CEO, COO and CFO and perhaps many others, get an inch-thick book of spreadsheets every month that show every detail of every project and every expense and every dollar of revenue. You know your break-even multipliers and your revenue multipliers and your multiple multipliers on a project basis, past month basis and a year-to-date basis. It's all there in glorious (or not-so-glorious) black and white.

But, what is in place to give incentive for people to help your fledgling new office? If your talented people back in HQ work on a not-so profitable project in your new branch, how will that person and his profit center be rewarded? Is there financial incentive to do so? If not, you will need to work with your CFO to put them in place.

A friend of mine who ran a branch office that competed with mine, couldn't get help from his HQ because his projects were generally not profitable enough for the help that he needed. In other words, folks back in his HQ wouldn't work on his projects because their profit center did not receive profit from the help that they gave. What a screwed-up system. They were beating themselves just due to some accounting system that could easily be changed if there was management attention to it.

The conflict here, is of course, that you and your CFO put your systems in place in order to track and incentivize your HQ profit centers. Now, put in an accounting system to make sure that your profit centers are encouraged to share work and expertise with your BO's. Can you do that?

Fundamental Truth No. 6 – you're always stepping on toes. Back in the HQ, you have experts leading various practice groups, right? You may have an HVAC group that does a great job of pushing air through a building. Or, you may have an airport design group that designs airports all over the planet; or, a food processing group or a cyber security group. Large firms have groups doing about everything imaginable. And, each practice group has several experts at doing that work.

> **Brilliant Advise Box**
>
> The real purpose of a branch office when it comes to sales, is to sell all work to *clients*. The reason the branch office is there is to develop relationships and trust with area clients. So, branches should sell everything that your company does to local clients, albeit with the help of experts back home.

Now suddenly, you have a new branch office that is out there selling work that those practice areas do, right? Your branch office is selling work and there's a very high probability that the work they are selling would normally be done by the appropriate group back at the HQ.

The difference is – now this is important – branch offices sell to *clients*. HQ groups sell services. Your food processing group calls on food processing companies nationwide or worldwide and tries to get food processing work from those companies who don't care if their work is done back at the HQ – right?

The opposite is true – or should be true – with branch offices. They exist *only* to sell work to clients who want their work done locally. Branch offices shouldn't care what services the local client needs – you'll do it with help as needed from HQ (or, experts in other BO's).

So, BO's sell *all* work done by your firm to local clients. At least that should be one of their objectives (see Objective Number 2b in Chapter 4). This means that all of the work they pursue will be stepping on the toes of the experts back at HQ. It's the job of the CEO and COO and VP of Marketing to make sure everyone gets along in the sandbox and are incentivized to work together.

Make sure your practice leaders back at HQ have on steel-toed boots that can take some stepping on as well as some incentive to help.

Chapter 6 – Selling Work

If you poll your principals, they will tell you the main reason to open a branch office. It is intuitively obvious to most that a new BO will not make much profit at first so the only other legitimate reason to invest in a new branch is to sell work that you are not now able to get.

Many (deep inside) want something similar to a minor-league system in Major League Baseball. Whenever they need a new player or some interesting work, they can just call on the minor-league team to help them out. And, whenever they've made a bad hiring decision, they can just send the bad hire to the minor-league team for training rather than fire them. Ok, I realize this is a pretty harsh accusation but undoubtedly, some of your division managers or profit center managers or principals, feel this way. Believe me, I know.

Think about this for a minute: it's the BO's main job, besides making money, to sell work to new, local clients. In order to do that, the BO must develop relationships with the decision-makers of those local clients. This takes many months or, even, years of relationship-making on both a personal and professional basis.

Branch offices, through their marketing folks and seller-doers, develop trust with local clients and then, when opportunities pop up, they then bring in the technical expertise necessary to sell and do the job, regardless of what it is. Does that make sense to you?

What the BO should *not* do is to hand over the client to the practice area that does that type of work. The BO wants to maintain and enhance the relationships that they have while providing the best technical work possible to their new, treasured client.

To that end, we often see that when an opportunity arises with a new client, the person in the BO that has the relationship with the new client serves as the project manager or "principal in charge" and brings in the experts required to do the work efficiently. This may fly in the face of the experts back in the HQ who are used to hunting their own game.

Each time the new client presents an opportunity, the BO should keep the same person in charge of the work and then bring in the appropriate practice people to help do it.

Branch offices sell everything your firm does to local clients who want their work done by a local firm. So, branch offices should *not* hand-over their new client to the experts back home but should get help from the experts back home to do work for your new client.

To go along with this, you should assign your senior people in the branch offices to be the client "manager" for your new clients. It is their job to continue to build relationships with them and to manage most or all of the work done for them. This is the way you build trust in each other. The senior person in your branch is responsible for getting the people necessary to do the work correctly and to "come through" for that new client.

Your new BO has a finite number of clients in their geographic area of influence – they can't afford to give them away. And, they can't afford to give them shoddy work.

I know a branch office that competed with mine who worked real hard for a couple of years to build relationships with a large, local private food processing company. The branch had a good local architectural and facilities practice. One day, the targeted company called and asked the company to do an environmental study for them.

> **Brilliant Advise Box**
>
> Your new branch office has a finite number of clients in their geographic area of influence. They can't afford to give them away nor can they afford to give them shoddy work.

The local office had no environmental expertise so they called the environmental folks back at HQ. So, the environmental folks set up a meeting, came to town and never involved anyone from the local office. They got the work and did it back at HQ.

A few weeks later, the same company called the *environmental group* with an opportunity to do some facilities work. So, of course, the environmental people handed it off to the facilities people in HQ and the local office was shut out of the targeted client, essentially, forever.

So, the best way to do work, at least at first, is to work together, led by the local folks who have the relationships and trust and bolstered by the experts from HQ who are going to make sure the work is done correctly, and, hopefully efficiently.

So, does all of this have to do with selling work? It's the preface for marketing work – it's the cart before the horse. You need to know how you're going to do the work before you sell the work. What is the culture of your org? How you do the work will depend mostly on how you sell the work.

How you sell work in your firm will depend on how work is sold in your branch offices, I presume. But, again, realize that your practice groups are used to selling their type of work nationally to clients who do their type of stuff.

Branch offices should be client-focused in their marketing activities and seek to get opportunities of any kind from their clients.

What does this mean? Branch offices should focus on marketing to clients in their geographic area of influence who need the kind of services your firm performs. It seems like I've said that before.

So, this means to me that your primary goal in selling work is to arrange for the decision-makers with potential clients to get to know and trust the key people in your branch office. I think selling work is probably the easiest activity of a new branch office. All of the other parts of running a business in a branch office are much harder.

Having said that, what are some ideas as to how to accomplish your marketing goals? Let's make a list again, but this time, just to be different, we'll do it A.B.C.....

    A. Do some market research as to who the potential clients are in your geographic area of influence. You already know quite a few potential or current clients but there are likely many more. There are a number of resources you can use to qualify your clients. Sorkins publishes a great directory that costs quite a bit to obtain, but may be worth it depending on how wide a swath you want to cover. Another source is D&B Hoovers. Digital versions of these directories can be sorted and tabulated in all sorts of ways.

You also have a much cheaper source and that would be the local newspaper that has articles every day as to what businesses and industries and agencies in town are doing what.

And, you may have now hired some local folks to help you out. They are a great source as to who the big clients are in town. Most will be obvious. You should have identified the top priority potential clients when you did your business plan for the new office. What may not be obvious is who the decision-makers are for those potential clients.

Make your own list and prioritize them based on whatever knowledge you have. Of course, put the clients at the top of your list who you are pretty sure need the services that your firm provides and who hire outside firms to do them.

B. Go see the people on your list. Call and make an appointment. Don't have your secretary (or, excuse me, your Executive Assistant) do it – no one likes to be one-upped by some jerk who can't bother to call you themselves. (I occasionally would get a call from someone who, after I said Hello, would say "Hold for Mr. Smith….". I would hang up immediately, of course, unless it was the President of the USA or the Queen of England….the person can call me themselves or pound sand.)

What are you trying to accomplish on your first and second and third visits with them? What you _don't_ want to do is give them a sales pitch. Forget that – if you do, they will start looking at their watch and usher you out the door. Rather, *listen* to them talk. They are dying to tell you about their company or agency and how much work they have coming up and how they select firms to outsource to.

Ask them:
1. What sort of services do they typically outsource?
2. Who are the decision-makers as to what work to outsource and to whom?
3. What is their process for selecting firms to outsource work to?
4. Who do they typically outsource work to? (i.e., who is your competition?)
5. What kind of work or projects do they have coming up?
6. Do they have preferences as to whether the work is done locally or not?
7. How can your firm get on their list of potential firms to outsource work to? Is there a form to fill out or will they accept a statement of qualifications?

C. In addition to these fundamental questions, you also want to find out personal information about the people in that org that are the decision-makers.

Find out things like: 1) where are they from; 2) where did they go to college; 3) what is their marital status; 4) what is their title and background; 4) what sorts of activities do they enjoy, i.e., the opera, soccer, Boy Scouts, hunting, running, etc.

You can find out most of these things during your visits to their office by looking around their office and noting photographs on display. You can see photos of their family (and ask about the names of their kids) and pics of them fishing in Mexico or riding a motorcycle as a Shriner in a parade, etc.

Remember, you need to get to know the person as well as the answers to the questions listed above. And, you need to let the person get to know you. Never tell them what you do at your firm or talk about your new branch office – at least not at first. Instead, relate to them things about your family and where you went to school and what you like to do in your spare time.

If you are not a good match, find someone in your org who is. For example, let's say your office manager is a young female and the decision-maker that you want to get to know is a male nearing retirement. You might have better luck getting to know him on a personal basis if you find someone more his age and gender.

D. Ok, now that you've met with your new, potential, decision-maker-client a few times, it may be time to invite him or her to lunch or to visit your office. Or, if you think you're ready, maybe invite the person to attend a soccer game. Here's an idea, invite him and his son to attend a baseball game with you and your son. Be a little creative. Or, there are many other venues, such as golf or a professional hockey game or a concert – make it something he will like.

Or, if you know him/her well enough, ask them and their spouse to join you and your spouse for dinner at a casual restaurant. I'm not a big fan of taking a client to a lavish restaurant or any lavish function. Remember, you are not trying to buy their vote or make them obligated to you, but to get to know each other so that he can trust you enough to hire you.

E. Here's some other ideas. After you have gotten to know this client through meetings in their office, giving them a tour of your office and maybe doing a social thing or two together, it's time to introduce some other folks in your branch to some folks in your client's org. Ask your newly-found buddy if he would be receptive to having a dinner some evening between some of the key people in your branch with some of the key people in the targeted org.

If possible, get your new buddy to invite them so that he is giving a subtle endorsement of your firm. At the dinner, have your chief electrical sit next to their chief electrical or your top roof expert sit next to their roof guy, or whatever. I would shoot for say, 12 at dinner – six or so from each company. It's up to you if you want to include cocktails (although it would normally be a must) and/or cigars at the end. Such a dinner is not too expensive but is a great way for your client's key people to get to know your key people.

Here's what *not* to do. **Never, under any circumstances**, include in the dinner a video of your company accomplishments or hand-out brochures or marketing pieces or whatever. This is a social occasion not a business meeting. If their folks want to know, they'll ask questions. Otherwise do *not* do a sales job: no presentations, no speeches, no lavish banquet, no bologna, no BS.

The other thing to be careful of doing is having folks attend from HQ. It's ok if you do, but make sure the folk or folks from HQ know what you are trying to do. Make sure *they* don't show up with a brochure or a video and hand out business cards with his phone number from HQ on it. I am not suggesting that you hide the fact that you may have some folks from HQ there but make sure that they understand that this is your party and they have to mind their manners.

Also, if you're going to do this, it's a good idea to have a company officer there. If your BO manager isn't one, it may be a good idea to invite one who is and who is going to be on your side.

F. You probably have your own ideas about marketing and how to get to know your clients. I like project picnics before, during and after a project (assuming you are still speaking to one another).

I also like to invite my clients to attend "internal" training sessions. If you're going to have a two-hour class on say, pump design, open it up to some of your clients. They will appreciate the offer and will give them the impression that you also are technically-minded as well as party-minded. This would go for any type of training, including sexual harassment training, or a cyber security course. It doesn't cost you anything and may get you a lot.

G. The last, best way to get to know your client, is to have them to your house for dinner – them and their spouse. Of course, this takes cooperation with your spouse, but you have now cemented your relationship if you can swing it.

The problem with these ideas is that you can't do this with 40 of your best clients. There are not enough days in the week. And, once in a while, you have a commitment other than work to attend to. You may have a kid or two running around your house that you need to say "hello" to once in a while.

So, you have to prioritize who you're going to do this with and perhaps get some help from your senior people, too. Like I said, your senior people ought to have, say, 10 clients that they are responsible for and they each could try to do these things with each of them.

I'm not going to insult your intelligence by advising you in this book on how to write a proposal or how to develop a brochure or put together an ad campaign. As we all know, but sometimes are afraid to admit, that is not how we get work anyway.

We get work from clients who trust us.

Trust us how?

They trust that we will:
    a. come through for them when times get rough;
    b. be honest and direct with them;
    c. give them quality work with experienced people;
    d. tell them the truth (see b, above);
    e. be the best value for them considering your price and the quality work you do and the service that you give.

By the way, while we are on the subject, I am not a fan of taking clients on fishing trips, golf weekends in Florida, or to expensive affairs. Do that at your own risk.

I am a fan of client entertainment as discussed above. But, again, the purpose of client entertainment is not to make the client obligated to you or to bribe them with a few NFL tickets. That never works, anyway.

Brilliant Advise Box

The purpose of client entertainment is to go with your client(s) to an event so that they can get to know and trust you as a person and as a professional.

The purpose of client entertainment is to go with your client(s) so that they can get to know you and trust you as a person and as a professional.

One more thing. When you do hand your client a brochure about your firm, make sure that the phone number and address on the brochure are *your* branch phone number and address. One time I was meeting with our fairly new corporate director of marketing who proudly showed me the new brochures that he had developed and that he wanted me (and our other branch offices) to hand out. Unfortunately, all of the brochures had the phone number and address of the headquarters printed on them. Sorry, Charlie, I'm not going to hand those out.

I want my clients to call me or someone in my branch office when they need something or have a question. How about you?

Chapter 7 - Organizing

Sometimes, it is difficult to establish an organizational structure for your new branch office. Branch offices are not, after all, practice divisions. Remember, they sell everything your company does to a limited number of clients in a limited geographic area. Branch offices should, nonetheless be profit centers.

So, the first big question is "Who does the Branch Manager report to?

There are a few choices.

First, the new branch manager might report to the COO or the CEO. If your firm has other BO's, do the managers of those all report to a single person? If so, then that's easy, your new BO manager will, likewise.

But, some firms have different BO managers reporting to different people. In those firms, branch offices are (wrongly) primarily focused on selling a single practice or service area so it makes some sense that the BO manager will end up reporting to the chief practice manager that they do work for. This happens a lot with branch offices that are started based on circumstances (remember? – one of the wrong reasons).

In those cases, the firm sold a project in a far-away land and convinced some schmuck back at HQ to go forth and open an office to be the "liaison" between the client and the project and folks back at HQ that are really doing the work. I call that a "project office", not to be confused with a real branch office. If you want your real branch office to grow and be a permanent part of the landscape, then make it a real branch office.

Ok, so your new branch office manager should report to a single person back at HQ who can be your advocate and supporter back home and who can deflect the slings and arrows that, undoubtedly, will be slung back in the HQ.

This person needs to "be on the side" as well as alongside the new branch office and understand its mission and objectives as well as the difficulties it faces. The person needs to read this book, of course.

This person might be in charge of all the branch office managers and in doing so travels to each one on a regular basis and works with the branch managers to help with moving work around, billable time, hiring decisions and, of course, helping to make the office highly profitable.

Whoever the person is that the new branch manager reports to needs to have the time and patience to spend time and energy with the branch offices. That's why I am normally opposed to the CEO or the COO being the boss of the branch managers, unless maybe, there is only one branch.

Early on, let's decide who is going to be the boss of the BO manager and then let's think about how we're going to organize below the BO manager.

In branch offices that are on the right track, there are several practice areas represented. Probably, each practice area is led by a go-getter who is working with the folks back at HQ on writing proposals and selling work and doing work. Who do these people report to? Do they report to the branch manager or to someone back in HQ in the practice area that they work in?

For example, a branch office of an architectural firm might have a group that designs clinics and hospitals and another group that designs schools and institutional buildings. They are marketing to those specific clients in their geographic area of influence and in doing so, don't forget, are also trying to get other kinds of work that the firm does.

Each of those groups may have a staff of architects that specialize in that type of work, and, even, some engineers to support their practice such as mechanical, electrical and structural engineers that they "share".

I have seen this work several ways. I know of firm that, in fact, doesn't even have a branch office manager. Each of the local practice leads report back to the Big Practice Lead back in HQ. The Big Practice Lead makes all of the marketing and contract decisions and decides what work the local folks are going to do and what they are not going to do.

They may do work on other projects far removed from their location while their counterparts in other branch locations may work on projects located in their neighborhood. This is certainly a streamlined approach but I am definitely not a fan of this method. The system is fraught with problems, primarily the problem of establishing silos erected back at HQ in the branches – a big mistake.

Someone needs to be in charge of the local clients and to make sure that the local folks are developing relationships with the local clients – that's why you're there, after all. Whoever employs the former method doesn't get it.

Some other companies that I know have the local lead practice folks report to the local branch manager. In fact, the local branch manager has final authority to hire, fire, sign contracts and decide who does what work. The local branch manager works with the local practice leads to make sure their people have good work to do and that the branch is client-based and not practice-based.

Does this make sense to you? It does to me. Otherwise just hire a clerk to pay the light bill each month and call it good.

Ultimately, you want the local branch manager to have control of all of the folks that work there. The branch manager, through his local managers, assigns work, does performance appraisals, establishes raises and promotions and bonuses, all within the guidelines of the company. The branch manager may want to consult with and work closely with the practice managers back at HQ. That would be a great idea.

Another organization item is to develop a menu of who can do what. This may already be done in your organization if you are a medium or large firm but if you are a small firm, maybe you haven't established yet, who can do what in your company.

What do I mean by that?

> **Brilliant Advise Box**
>
> Your new branch office practice leaders should report directly to the branch manager, not the practice leaders back in HQ. In fact, all of the people in your firm that works in the branch location should report, directly or indirectly, to the branch manager.

Who can negotiate and execute a contract in your branch offices? Many firms stipulate that a "principal" or officer must execute contracts, which normally means that person is also authorized to negotiate the deal.

Or, perhaps, the contract must be approved in form back at the HQ by a legal staff member and/or a risk management lead and/or by the CFO and/or the insurance manager and/or the COO. I would think that your branch manager ought to have the authority to negotiate the terms of the contract as well as to execute it, provided that the contract conforms to certain guidelines stipulated by the CEO/COO.

To me, it looks suspicious to a client if the person executing the contract isn't the local head person. If the local branch manager or the local practice manager can't negotiate and execute a contract, then maybe I'm talking to the wrong person or, maybe, the wrong firm.

If you have relocated your new branch manager from HQ to open and run a new branch office then you ought to trust the newly promoted BOM enough to make him or her a principal or officer in the firm – that ought to be part of the package.

For sure, the BOM needs to follow the rules established by the CEO/COO regarding insurance requirements and liability language. And, there may be a limit to the amount of the contracts the new BOM is authorized to sign.

How about another list? Let's look at things that the branch manager can and should do, with input, of course from the appropriate people from HQ:

What Branch Managers Should Do:
1. Lead & manage sales locally
2. Establish sales goals
3. Make "Go – No Go" Decisions
4. Establish costs for a project.
5. Manage preparation and/or produce and sign proposals.
6. Produce work, i.e. be part of a production team
7. Manage work, i.e. project manager and production team
8. Assemble production teams
9. Check quality of work
10. Determine and manage risk

11. Negotiate and execute contract documents
12. Develop and execute business plans
13. Determine and monitor manpower needs
14. Manage growth
15. Hire and terminate employees
16. Manage careers and professional development
17. Approve expense reports
18. Prepare and mail invoices
19. Check invoices
20. Receive payments through a local lock box
21. Be a profit/loss center
22. Develop a national reputation in specific area(s).

Are there any other things? I'm sure there are. Of course, the above activities must be done within the rules and culture of the firm. For example, the local branch manager should have ultimate hiring responsibility but should work with the firm's HR group to make sure offers and signing bonuses, etc. are in line with the firm's policies and that they are consistent with good non-discrimination practices.

It's important for the firm as well as the local branch managers to know who they work for and what the organizational guidelines are for running the office.

Chapter 8 – Measuring Performance

What sorts of financial reporting does your firm have? I hope that it is comprehensive and shared with your principals each month. Is it? Many firms, especially small partnerships or sole-proprietors, keep financial information pretty close to their vest. That's ok, but you have to consider how your key people are incentivized to out-perform.

As I have said *many* times in this book, I very firmly believe that branch offices should be set up as profit centers on day one. Everyone needs to know what that office is costing or how much money they are making. Have you bought into that yet? The financials for each of your branch offices should be set up in the same way as your practice or product divisions.

Measure your branches in the same way as you measure your other profit centers. What do you measure?
      a. Revenue
      b. Costs
      c. Expenses
      d. Sales
      e. Marketing expenses
      f. Profit or loss
      g. Profit or loss per person
      h. Break-even multiplier
      i. Effective Multiplier
      j. Salary overheads
      k. Office overheads
      l. Corporate overheads
      m. Staff size
      n. Billability or Net Billable Time
      o. Accounts Receivable
      p. Receivable Days
      q. Total Days

    r. Taxes paid
    s. And, so on, and on, and on

With these and many other measures, your profit center managers can digest how they can make more profit. How do they measure up with their counterparts? How does their net billable time measure against other profit centers?

How do their office overheads compare against other profit centers and other branch offices? What are their monthly expenses compared to others? Are they spending too much on sales and marketing? Is their effective multiplier too low? If so, they need to price their work higher. Can they lower their expenses and make more profit? Or, can they increase their pricing and make more profit? Or, both?

I am a believer in providing this information on a monthly basis to each of your profit centers and including all of the data for each profit center. Of course, you will need to encourage security of those documents.

Your branch managers must know how they are measured and must be able to see how they compare with other profit centers and other branch offices. I call that incentive.

Ok, hopefully by now you are convinced that branch offices and branch office managers and your people in branch offices must be measured and compared with others. Right? Are you on board yet?

Now what? How might branch managers and the people in your branch offices be compensated and incentivized so that they continue to aspire to make your branch office(s) more profitable per shareholder than your other profit centers. That's our only good reason to open an office and the number 1 goal of an office, right? How are they doing in that regard?

I will tell you (again) that it is normally much more difficult to make a profit in a branch office than it is in a headquarters-based practice center or profit center. Those HQ folks have been around for a long time and have a very good "infrastructure" of people who know how to price work and make money and to do quality work. Your branches and their managers are still learning that.

Your branch managers need to understand what their goals are. Yes, their primary goal is to make more profit per shareholder than the rest of the company. But, exactly, how to do that? Your BOMs need to understand what their net billable time goal is and their office overhead goal. And, their sales goals in different practice areas. They just absolutely cannot achieve their main, Number 1 goal, without understanding what it takes to get there.

Let's hope that your branch office will dig for water and find gold, but most won't. Most will struggle to sell work and to do work efficiently and to follow your quality control program and to hire quality people and to sell profitable work. Over time, they will get better at it *if* you give them the information that they need.

Remember M. CEO, this is your money you are spending – help your investment prosper by measuring them and letting them see it.

Chapter 9 – Quality Control

You have a company QC program...surely. If you don't, go back and read Chapter 1. You have no business opening a branch office if you don't have a company QC program. So, ok, you have one.

But, it may not address QC in branch offices. Most companies with branch offices have a QC program wherein work is checked back at the HQ by qualified professionals. Or, if the branch has plenty of qualified professionals itself, then those folks should be the ones checking work.

Likely, each branch office has someone appointed to be the branch QC manager. If you have a branch office or two that do not have a QC manager assigned.....oops. That needs to be fixed right away. It goes without saying that this person should be appointed at the start of the office and they need to take their duties very seriously. The person should have deep knowledge of the company QC program and should be authorized to make sure that the branch follows it when they do their work. The person would work closely with the overall company QC director and report directly to the branch manager.

Well, that much is simple and pretty logical. No problem.

Quality control programs normally include checking work by someone not otherwise involved in the project or assignment who is qualified and considered an expert in the area of the work. In many cases, this person or persons may actually do quality control checks on nearly a full-time basis. Or, as a senior professional, they do a lot of checking and correcting, if necessary.

Your new branch office will eventually have some seasoned professionals in it who are qualified to check the work of your branch, or, at least the work for which the person is qualified.

My suggestion is this: rather than have this qualified person or persons check work for the branch office, send work from the

HQ to this person to check and, at the same time, send work from the branch to appropriate HQ people to check. In this way, there is a cross-check as well as transferring knowledge of how the company QC program works from HQ to the branch and vice-versa.

I tried to get this accomplished on many occasions with no luck but I still think it's a great idea. It might take some executive direction and certainly some buy-in from the company QC manager. Frankly, in some cases, the folks in the HQ don't feel comfortable having their work checked in a BO. Why? Yet, branch office people are supposed to feel fine having their work checked in HQ.

And, it's a great idea to follow up and find out who in the HQ is checking your branch office work. Are they qualified? Or, is it just someone who needs some billable work to do? Stop questioning me – I've seen it happen.

I had an instance when my branch office was overloaded with work and I requested a certain senior person who I knew well to travel to my branch and to help out with doing some work, including doing some QC checking in his field. He did come and help out. At that time, he had been with the company for around 25 years and was considered an expert in his field.

> **Brilliant Advise Box**
>
> If your company QC program isn't working very well, I'd firstly change-out your director of quality control and then find out why and then, have your new director fix it.

When he arrived, I asked him if he would attend a quality review session for one of our projects, for which he was qualified. I told him that I wanted him to participate for his expertise as well as to help the other folks there see and learn how quality reviews were done back at headquarters. He told me he would be happy to attend but he couldn't help much with showing us how to do one as he had never participated in one. I was dumb-founded. I was indazzled (i.e., dazzled in a negative way – like famous and infamous). How could this be? Well, it "be" because as it turns out the group he was assigned to didn't follow the company QC program worth a dam (oops, QC check needed).

So, we were able to show him how we followed the company QC program in a branch office. I was a little embarrassed for him, but deeply embarrassed for his practice area back at the head-shed.

If your quality control program isn't working, you really ought to find out why and revitalize it. I'd start with getting a new company QC director that either has the time or commitment to make it happen. Too often, companies name their big techno-nerd type person to the position of company QC director or office QC manager or practice area QC manager.

This person is brilliant but sometimes has no leadership or managerial ability. I think you need a good people-person in this position who can get your company, including your branch offices, to follow the QC program. Don't you?

This is a pretty short chapter because it's pretty simple stuff. If you have a company QC program, make sure it is written for and doable by your branch offices. If it isn't, re-write it. If you don't have one, get one up and running before you open your first branch office.

Chapter 10 – Risk Management

Ouch. We really don't want to talk about risk when it comes to branch offices. They are certainly out of site, so let's just accept them as "out of mind" and hope for the best. After all, you're covered by all kinds of insurance. Although we don't want to make a claim, we do have to accept some risks if we are going to move forward and in order to move forward, we need to have efficient, growing, profitable branch offices.

You have a risk manager, right? In smaller companies, it may be you. Certainly, the CEO and COO are ultimately the top risk managers in the company. But, you do have some sort of risk manager in addition to the CEO and COO. You may have a real, full-time risk manager; or, you may have a full-time attorney or an insurance manager; or, at least, an attorney on retainer who serves as your consultant on risk mitigation.

Have you talked to them about risk management in branch offices? They would be a good source. In fact, you might ask them to review your risk management policies, if you have them, to see if operating a branch office fits into those policies. If not, you might ask them to edit your policies so that branch offices know where they fit.

Regardless of your size or sophistication regarding risk management, your branch office managers need to understand the CEO/COO's risk aversion.

Firstly, your BOM needs to understand the company insurance plan and what policies your firm has, but that's easy.

What kind of work do you *not* want to do? I know a firm that shies away from doing work for churches. Historically, churches don't have much money and it is difficult to make a profit when doing work for a church.

> **Brilliant Advise Box**
>
> Risk managers are doing their job if the company never goes after any project. No projects; no risk. But, you cannot run a business that way.

85

That's the kind of risk "policy", even if not in writing, that the branch managers need to know about.

Some companies establish a policy that all proposals from a branch office to a client must be approved by appropriate people back in HQ before being submitted. In this way, the potential project is screened and projects that may have too much risk to swallow, will be rejected before a proposal is submitted. Personally, I think that's an awful way to address risk.

Alternately, let's give the branch office manager the knowledge of the risk tolerance of the company so that the branch manager is as risk averse as the executive management. Let the branch manager decide if the project is too risky or in what ways the company may be able to offset the risk.

If I were a branch manager who spent two years courting a client and building relationships and gaining trust and finally getting a shot to do a project, only for some yo-yo back at the HQ to nix the deal, I would be furious. Risk managers, of course, have nothing to lose.

Risk managers are doing their job if the firm doesn't go after any projects. No projects – no risk.

I would establish a menu of items that might trigger a risk review for a potential project for the company. For example, if your project scope of work stipulates that you will be paid in currency other than US dollars, then that would trigger a risk review which might consider ways to mitigate that risk or might mean the firm is not willing to take the risk at all.

There would be many other triggers, such as:
- a. A proposed contract having a warrantee or guarantee different than your firm normally accepts.
- b. A project located in a foreign country.
- c. A project that might have insurance requirements different than your firm carries.
- d. A project for which the contract has untenable liability terms.

    e. A project for which the contract includes liquidated damages.
    f. A project that includes a scope of work for which your firm has no experience.
    g. A project for a church.

You get the idea. Your risk management people can give you additional risk menu items. Make this menu available to principals in your firm and so that if any project they are pursuing includes any these items, the project has to go through a risk review before a binding proposal is submitted.

The purpose of the risk review is not to nix the deal but to find out how the firm might be able to mitigate the risk and what it will cost to do so. Then, whether to proceed is a business decision based on potential profit and known costs.

Bob's Top Ten

There may be quite a lot in this book that you disagree with. I knew a boss once that always said, "…if you don't agree with 80% of what I do, then you ought to leave….".

So, here's my top ten things to do regarding branch offices. I hope you agree with at least eight.

1. Make your branch offices profit centers on day one. The principals and partners and board members and branch managers need to see their financials and to see them monthly. They need to be able to compare their numbers with the other profit centers and understand what it takes to make money.
2. Your branch offices' primary reason to exist is that the company will make more profit per shareholder with them than without them, at least in the medium to long term. If that's not your primary reason for opening a branch office, then you shouldn't.
3. Their second reason to exist is to develop relationships and trust with new potential clients in your area.
4. Some clients will only hire service firms or purchase products made locally and they want their work to be done locally. They are the target of a branch office. Other clients will hire firms regardless of where they are located. You don't need a branch office to sell work to these companies – think Amazon.
5. Clients hire firms to work with because they trust one firm more than they trust others. Clients don't hire firms based on qualifications, marketing brochures, websites, presentations or cost. They hire them because they trust them and you have to have a relationship with someone in order to trust them.
6. Headquarters will almost always be able to do work with more efficiency and more quality and at a lower cost, than a branch office. You have to be able to accept this if you want to be in the branch office business.
7. A major objective of a branch office ought to be growth. You have to have work in order to grow. You have to let

branch offices do most of the work that they sell or they won't grow, regardless of the toes you're stepping on.
8. Branch managers should report to someone at headquarters who will be their advocate and sponsor. Everyone else in a branch office city should report directly or indirectly to the branch manager.
9. The location of a branch office is not all that important. What is important is who you get to run your office, how they are incentivized and how they are supported back at HQ.
10. Branch offices sell to a finite number of local clients. Branches should sell all of services that your company does to local firms and then get help doing the work from the practice areas of the firm. If your branch office is only selling one service to a few existing clients, then that is a "project" office, not a branch office. Project offices exist to finish the project and close. Branch offices exist for the long haul.

www.ingramcontent.com/pod-product-compliance
Lightning Source LLC
Chambersburg PA
CBHW052335220526
45472CB00001B/429